4.4.78

Prayers for Families

Barbara Owen Webb

Judson Press ® Valley Forge

For Tricia, Jeffie, and Steve

PRAYERS FOR FAMILIES

Printed in the U.S.A.

Suggestions for Using This Book

Each family will discover for itself a variety of ways for using these prayers according to the needs and makeup of the family. But a few thoughts are offered here for your consideration. You will notice these are "we" prayers to be used whenever two or more are gathered together, rather than "I" prayers for personal devotions. The reason for this is to encourage the family members at home to come together before God, to find a special kind of oneness praying together.

The prayers are short. Often, time is short, or so it seems. These prayers may be used in the early morning rush when we're tempted to say there's no time. Using one of the morning prayers, a parent and child may pause for prayer before the child goes off to school.

At a more relaxed time, when the whole family is together, perhaps you'll have family devotions. You may read a selection from the Bible or a devotional book, sing a hymn, have a prayer. One of the prayers in this book could be read as the prayer or used as a "starter" to which spontaneous prayer or silent prayer could be added. A word should be said about silent prayer in the family group. It can be especially useful both at those times when children become self-conscious about praying aloud in their own words and as training for them in being still before the Lord. Also, some families hold hands around the table when they pray—both a restraint to busy fingers and a blessed bond.

It is hoped that this book will be kept where it will be available to all in the household, and the children may know that in this book there is a prayer for the snowy day, boring day, or grouchy day. When the day comes, they will use the appropriate prayer with that special satisfaction which comes from knowing that someone else has shared the experience. (Isn't that one reason we all enjoy written prayers at times—to know that someone else has felt the way we feel and has put it into words?)

The Scripture is included with each prayer to help children realize what a treasure of assurance we have in God's Word. Before we ever spoke to God, he spoke to us. His Word is clear about his great love for us. We can pray about anything in our lives. From his Word we see how interested he is in all we do and everything about us.

A final note about the blank pages. These were suggested by my son when I asked for his ideas for this book. "Have some blank pages to write your own prayers," he said, "or people could write down stuff they're praying about." So we've included these pages for your prayers or prayer requests which you want to remember.

May this little book prove a blessing to *your* family.

Barbara Owen Webb

Contents

Morning
and evening
prayers

Sunday Morning Prayer

Dear Lord, you have kept us this night. We thank you.

You forgive us and make us new for this new day. We praise you.

Please be with us all day long just as you have promised. We love you.

In Jesus' name. Amen.

FROM GOD'S WORD—

[Jesus said,] ". . . I will be with you always, to the end of the age."

Matthew 28:20

Sunday Evening Prayer

Dear God, the day is over. We thank you for its blessings.
The night is coming. We ask sweet rest in your care.
Bless all in this house all through the night.

In Jesus' name. Amen.

FROM GOD'S WORD—

He made the sun and the moon;
his love is eternal;
the sun to rule over the day;
his love is eternal;
the moon and the stars to rule over the night;
his love is eternal.

Psalm 136:7-9

Monday Morning Prayer

O Lord, we begin this day knowing that we have much to do. Help us in doing these things.

Bless us; bless our tasks. We thank you already, Lord.

In Jesus' name. Amen.

From God's Word—

May our Lord Jesus Christ himself and God our Father . . . encourage you and strengthen you to always do and say what is good.

2 Thessalonians 2:16-17

Monday Evening Prayer

Dear God, use the work we did today; bless the people we met today; forgive the wrongs we did today.

Thank you for our play; thank you for our home and food. Thank you most of all for our Savior, Jesus.

In his name. Amen.

From God's Word—

May the Lord show his constant love during the day,
so that I may have a song at night,
a prayer to the God of my life.

Psalm 42:8

Tuesday Morning Prayer

Thank you, heavenly Father, for keeping us in your care all night. We thank you especially for our Savior, Jesus, who makes us your children. For his sake help us to love; help us to share; help us to be kind today.

Amen.

From God's Word—

You are the people of God; he loved you and chose you for his own. So then, you must clothe yourselves with compassion, kindness, humility, gentleness, and patience.

Colossians 3:12

Tuesday Evening Prayer

O Lord, we have finished our work for this day. We will rest in your care.

Please watch over us all night long while we sleep.

For Jesus' sake. Amen.

From God's Word—

When I lie down, I go to sleep in peace;
you alone, O Lord, keep me perfectly safe.

Psalm 4:8

Wednesday Morning Prayer

Dear Lord, here we are ready for the new day. Go with us, we pray. Be our guide and protector. Help us to share your love with others, especially those who do not know you.

Then bring us safely together again in the evening.

We ask in Jesus' name. Amen.

FROM GOD'S WORD—

But you are . . . God's own people, chosen to proclaim the wonderful acts of God, who called you out of darkness into his own marvelous light.

1 Peter 2:9

Wednesday Evening Prayer

Dear God, we come to you at the end of this day. Bless the good things we have done. Forgive the wrong. Comfort people everywhere who are sad or lonely or sick.

Keep us in your loving care this night. We rest, knowing that you are here.

In Jesus' name. Amen.

FROM GOD'S WORD—

"I will comfort them and turn their mourning
into joy,
their sorrow into gladness.
I will . . .
. . . satisfy all the needs of my people.
I, the Lord, have spoken."

Jeremiah 31:13*b*-14

Thursday Morning Prayer

Dear Lord, you have always been good to us. We know that you will be good to us today. Thank you already.

Show your goodness to all our relatives everywhere. Bless the people in our schools and where we work. Have mercy on those who are sick.

And please make us blessings to every person we meet today.

For Jesus' sake. Amen.

FROM GOD'S WORD—

The Lord's unfailing love and mercy still continue,
Fresh as the morning, as sure as the sunrise.
Lamentations 3:22-23

Thursday Evening Prayer

Dear heavenly Father, thank you for this day. Thank you for this moment when we can give you our problems and praise you for our joys. In this quiet evening, help us to feel quiet and peaceful because you are here and love us forever.

In Jesus' name. Amen.

FROM GOD'S WORD—

[Jesus said,] "Peace is what I leave with you; it is my own peace that I give you."

John 14:27*a*

Friday Morning Prayer

Dear Lord, on this Friday morning, be with us in all we do.

The week is getting old, but the day is new.
Help us to use it for you.

In Jesus' name we pray. Amen.

From God's Word—

Trust in the Lord with all your heart. Never rely on what you think you know. Remember the Lord in everything you do, and he will show you the right way.

Proverbs 3:5-6

Friday Evening Prayer

We thank you for this day, Lord. We thank you for work to do and time to play. We thank you for laughter. We thank you, too, for tears that help to wash away our hurts. We thank you most for Jesus, our Savior, who takes away our sins.

In his name. Amen.

From God's Word—

And God showed his love for us by sending his only Son into the world, so that we might have life through him.

1 John 4:9

Saturday Morning Prayer

Dear Father in heaven, thank you for refreshing sleep. Thank you for this brand-new day. Thank you for our loving Savior, Jesus.

Help us today to bring his love to all we meet.

We are ready.

Amen.

FROM GOD'S WORD—

May you always be joyful in your union with the Lord. I say it again: rejoice!

Philippians 4:4

Saturday Evening Prayer

O Lord, how great and wonderful you are! You forgive our sins. You are with us all day long and all night, too. We thank you and ask your blessings for others. Please bless our neighbors, our relatives, and friends. Bless people everywhere for this night.

For Jesus' sake. Amen.

FROM GOD'S WORD—

May the Lord bless you and take care of you;
May the Lord be kind and gracious to you;
May the Lord look on you with favor and give you peace.

Numbers 6:24-26

A page for your prayers

Occasional
prayers

Before Church

Dear heavenly Father, bless our time in church today. Open our ears to hear your Word. Open our lips to sing your praises. Open our hearts that your love may come in.

Then open our hands to serve.

In Jesus' name. Amen.

From God's Word—

"But the word of the Lord remains forever."
This word is the Good News that was proclaimed to you.

1 Peter 1:25

On Beginning the School Year

Dear Lord, it's the first day of school. Go with us and give us understanding. Be with our teachers, too. Give them wisdom and patience and joy. Dear Lord, bless our learning; bless our day; bless our year.

In Jesus' name. Amen.

From God's Word—

[The Lord] will protect you as you come and go
now and forever.

Psalm 121:8

When the First Robin Comes

Dear God, the first robin came today. Thank you. We know that spring will soon be here. We thank you.

Bless all the little birds that sing to us of your love. Fill us, too, with spring joy.

In Jesus' name. Amen.

FROM GOD'S WORD—

Sing a new song to the Lord;
he has done wonderful things!
Psalm 98:1*a*

On a Snowy Day

Dear God, thank you for snow. It's fun. It's beautiful. It's tingly cold. We love it and we thank you.

But some people don't love it, God. Help the people who have to drive in it or work outside in it. Keep them safe, and help them to see how pretty it is—even if some of them don't think it's fun.

Come, Lord Jesus, outside with us while we play.

Amen.

FROM GOD'S WORD—

At God's command amazing things happen,
wonderful things that we can't understand.
He commands snow to fall on the earth.
Job 37:5-6*a*

In a Time of Sadness

We are sad today, Lord Jesus. You know how we feel because there were times when you were sad, too. It's hard to do things when you're sad.

Comfort us. Wipe away our tears. Be close to each of us, and give us rest and peace.

Amen.

FROM GOD'S WORD—

The Lord is near to those who are discouraged;
he saves those who have lost all hope.

Psalm 34:18

On the Death of a Pet

O God, our dog (cat, gerbil, etc.) died today. Help us not to feel so lonely. He was such a special dog.

Thank you for making dogs. Thank you for all the good times we had with him. Let our memories cheer up our hearts.

Come close, Lord Jesus. Amen.

FROM GOD'S WORD—

Then the Lord God said, "It is not good for the man to live alone. I will make a suitable companion to help him." So he took some soil from the ground and formed all the animals and all the birds. Then he brought them to the man to see what he would name them. . . .

Genesis 2:18-19

We're Moving, Lord

We're moving, Lord. We thank you for our home where we have lived. We thank you for friends and neighbors here, for streets and trees and mailboxes.

Things will be different when we move. A new home, new neighbors, new streets—all new to us. But old to you, Lord. You know our new home and our new neighborhood. You're already there. Prepare our way, Lord.

We thank you for the old. Now we thank you for the new, too.

In Jesus' name. Amen.

From God's Word—

If I flew away beyond the east
    or lived in the farthest place in the west,
you [,Lord,] would be there to lead me,
    you would be there to help me.

Psalm 139:9-10

On a Boring Day

Father, forgive us for feeling bored in your beautiful world. It's one of those days when there's nothing to do, nothing which is fun anyway.

Open our eyes and ears to what's happening around us today. You put surprises in our days. Help us not to miss them today.

In Jesus' name. Amen.

From God's Word—

Praise the Lord! . . .
Praise him for the mighty things he has done. . . .
Praise him with trumpets
    Praise him with harps and lyres.
Praise him with drums and dancing. . . .
    Praise him with loud cymbals.
Praise the Lord, all living creatures!
    Praise the Lord!

Psalm 150

A Prayer for Our Family

O heavenly Father, it is good to be part of a family. We thank you for each other. We share happy times and unhappy times. We share work and play. We are glad that we are not alone. You have put us in a family.

Please bless us now. Keep giving us your love to share with each other.

In the name of Jesus, your Son and our Savior. Amen.

FROM GOD'S WORD—

Sing to God, sing praises to his name.
He gives the lonely a home to live in.
Psalm 68:4*a*, 6*a*

Thanks for Our New Baby

Dear Jesus, we thank you for our new baby. Help us to remember that once each of us was a baby. We cried and wiggled, ate and slept, as our new baby does.

Someone cared for us. Now help us to care for our baby. Help us to teach [him/her] of you.

Amen.

FROM GOD'S WORD—

We will tell the next generation
about the Lord's power and his great deeds
and the wonderful things he has done.
Psalm 78:4*b*

When a Child Is Sick

O Jesus. [child's name] is sick today. Be with [him/her]. Comfort [him/her]. Give [child's name] your special attention just as you did to children long ago.

We thank you and praise your name. Amen.

FROM GOD'S WORD—

Then [Jesus] took the children in his arms, placed his hands on each of them, and blessed them.

Mark 10:16

When Mother (or Father) Is Sick

Dear God, Mother is sick today. Please help her to feel better. Be special to her now. She is always special to us when we are sick.

Help us to be helpers today. Keep us cheerful, and fill us with your love to share with our mother.

In Jesus' name. Amen.

FROM GOD'S WORD—

May you be made strong with all the strength which comes from his glorious power, so that you may be able to endure everything with patience.

Colossians 1:11

Mother Has a New Job

Things are different at our house, Lord. Mother has a new job. Bless her.

Bless us, too. Make us all helpers to each other. Give us family joy in this new way of doing things.

We pray in Jesus' name. Amen.

FROM GOD'S WORD—

Charm is deceptive and beauty disappears, but a woman who honors the Lord should be praised.

Give her credit for all she does. She deserves the respect of everyone.

Proverbs 31:30-31

Father Has a New Job

O Lord, Father has a new job. We thank you for it and ask your blessing on him and his work. Help us to be helpful to him while he is busy learning all the new things about this new job.

Through this work please bless our family that we may be blessings to others.

In Jesus' name. Amen.

FROM GOD'S WORD—

Do not forget to do good and to help one another, because these are the sacrifices that please God.

Hebrews 13:16

On a Grouchy Day

Dear Lord, it's been one of those grouchy days. We have grumbled at each other. Forgive us. We have shouted at each other. Forgive us.

Thank you, Lord. Now we can be kind again. Keep making us new for the rest of the day. Keep grouchiness away, and give us your love for each other.

In Jesus' name. Amen.

FROM GOD'S WORD—

Happy are those whose sins are forgiven,
whose wrongs are pardoned.

Psalm 32:1

After a Difficult Day

Dear Father in heaven, we're so glad that we can call you "Father," especially after a day like today. It was a hard day, a tiring day. So much went wrong.

Thank you for loving us enough to hear our complaints. Thank you for putting us in a family where we have each other. Thank you for this quiet time together with you. Forgive us; bless us; and give us your peace.

We ask in Jesus' name. Amen.

FROM GOD'S WORD—

Praise the Lord,
who carries our burdens day after day;
he is the God who saves us.

Psalm 68:19

A page for your prayers

Holiday prayers

First Sunday in Advent

O Lord, we thank you today for the prophets you sent in Old Testament times. We thank you for Jeremiah and Isaiah and all the others who told that one day your Son would come. Help us during this Advent season to keep our thoughts on Jesus, just as the prophets did long ago.

In Jesus' name. Amen.

From God's Word—

. . . Isaiah replied, "Listen, now, . . . the Lord himself will give you a sign: a young woman who is pregnant will have a son and will name him 'Immanuel.'"

Isaiah 7:13-14

Second Sunday in Advent

Dear Lord, when you sent your Son, Bethlehem was not ready for him. He had to sleep on straw in a manger. Lord, make our hearts more ready than that. As we think about Jesus during this Advent season, help us to welcome him into our hearts.

In his name we ask this. Amen.

From God's Word—

. . . Christ will make his home in your hearts through faith.

Ephesians 3:17*a*

Third Sunday in Advent

Dear Lord, thank you for the shepherds of long ago who came to see the baby Jesus. In the busy town of Bethlehem they found the newborn Savior.

In this busy time before Christmas, may we find Jesus in all our preparations.

In his name. Amen.

From God's Word—

The shepherds went back, singing praises to God for all they had heard and seen; it had been just as the angel had told them.

Luke 2:20

Fourth Sunday in Advent

Dear heavenly Father, thank you for sending angels to announce the birth of your Son.

Help us to be like those angels, praising you and telling others that Jesus really came.

For his sake. Amen.

From God's Word—

But the angel said to them, "Don't be afraid! I am here with good news for you, which will bring great joy to all the people. This very day in David's town your Savior was born—Christ the Lord!"

Luke 2:10-11

Christmas Day

O Lord, how much you love us! You sent your Son to live on earth. We thank you. He showed us how kind and gentle you are. We praise you. He took away our sins. We thank you and celebrate this happy day.

Happy birthday, dear Jesus. Amen.

From God's Word—

For God loved the world so much that he gave his only Son, so that everyone who believes in him may not die but have eternal life. For God did not send his Son into the world to be its judge, but to be its savior.

John 3:16-17

New Year's Day

O great Lord, it's 19__. There is excitement in beginning a new year. Fat new calendars are waiting to be used.

But we stop a moment and thank you for the old year. Thank you for being with us every day and every night. Now forgive our sins, and make us as new as the new year.

In Jesus' name. Amen.

From God's Word—

"Listen!" says Jesus.". . . I am the first and the last, the beginning and the end."

Revelation 22:12*a*-13

Jesus Christ is the same yesterday, today, and forever.

Hebrews 13:8

Ash Wednesday

O Lord, forgive us for forgetting you so often. Help us during Lent to remember why Jesus died. We are sorry for our sins. Help us to live as your kind and loving children.

For Jesus' sake. Amen.

From God's Word—

"But even now," says the Lord,
"repent sincerely and return to me. . . ."
Come back to the Lord your God.
He is kind and full of mercy;
he is patient and keeps his promise;
he is always ready to forgive and not punish.

Joel 2:12-13

Maundy Thursday

Dear Lord, we remember that many, many years ago, on this night, Jesus gave us the Lord's Supper, Holy Communion. We thank you for this very special way to be with him and to remember all that he means to us.

We thank you in his name. Amen.

From God's Word—

In the same way, after the supper he took the cup and said, "This cup is God's new covenant, sealed with my blood. Whenever you drink it, do so in memory of me."

1 Corinthians 11:25

Good Friday

Heavenly Father, we stand in awe of what Jesus did for us. So often we quarrel and are mean or unkind. For these sins and the sins of all the world Jesus died. We are sorry for our sins. We rest in your care, knowing that you forgive us for the sake of Jesus, our Savior, who died on the cross.

Amen.

From God's Word—

"He willingly gave his life
and shared the fate of evil men.
He took the place of many sinners
and prayed that they might be forgiven."

Isaiah 53:12*b*

Easter

O Lord, Jesus is risen. The power and the glory are yours forever. We rejoice! We are your children forever and ever because of Jesus Christ, our Savior.

Hallelujah! Amen.

From God's Word—

[The angel said,] "I know you are looking for Jesus, who was crucified. He is not here; he has been raised, just as he said."

Matthew 28:5*b*-6*a*

Fourth of July

Heavenly Father, we praise you and thank you for the United States of America. Bless our country today on her birthday. Make our nation a joy to you and a blessing to others.

In Jesus' name. Amen.

From God's Word—

Righteousness makes a nation great; sin is a disgrace to any nation.

Proverbs 14:34

Thanksgiving Day

O God, can we ever thank you enough? For big things—land, sky, elephants—we thank you. For little things—rosebuds, sand, kittens—we thank you. For "people-made" things—buildings, cars, clothes—we thank you. For food and friends, parents and children, we thank you. For all these things we thank you now.

And for Jesus, our Savior, we thank you forever.

Amen.

From God's Word—

Let the giving of thanks be your sacrifice to God,
and give the Almighty all that you promised.

Psalm 50:14

A page for your prayers